LAURIE BETH JONES

JESUS
LIFE COACH

JOURNAL

Training Your Life

COUNTRYMAN
®

NASHVILLE, TENNESSEE

Project Editor: Kathy Baker

Designed by Lookout Design Group, Inc., Minneapolis, Minnesota

ISBN 1-4041-0180-2

www.jcountryman.com
www.thomasnelson.com

www.lauriebethjones.com

INTRODUCTION

WHETHER I AM MEETING with the president of
Wal–Mart or the officers of the U.S. Naval Academy in Annapolis,
I know the one question that is most on their minds is this: "How
can I coach others toward their highest and best?"

After spending a lifetime studying the character of Jesus, and
the better part of my career working with leaders, I have come to
this conclusion—there is no better role model than Jesus of
Nazareth for coaching that gets lasting results. This journal is one
of my contributions toward the profound gift and skill set known
as coaching, and it is designed as a tool to help you personally
draw out the kingdom within you.

Fulfillment is beyond "success." Knowing the difference
will determine what roads and what actions you choose to take
throughout the day. The shift of a few inches either way can make

all the difference. With Jesus as your Coach, you will begin to experience unbounded joy in his presence, no matter what. You will become more of a voice, rather than an echo, and daily will begin to paint what you love. You will have new stories to tell, as well as a renewed self–image. You will learn to be comfortable in a future state.

Research conducted by Harvard researcher Gerald Zaltman and described in his book *What Customers Think* revealed that we want people and organizations who will . . .

> save us time,
> be a resource for new ideas,
> connect with us relationally, and
> stay with us on the journey, through all its twists and turns.

Jesus is that person.

Welcome to your new Coach and the journal designed as a companion piece for your journey.

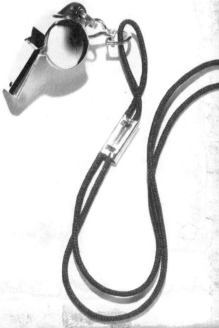

MY FRIEND JOE MATTHEWS shared a poignant story with me recently. His best friend's wife was diagnosed with terminal cancer and given a short time to live. Joe said he watched in awe as Dan and his wife, Christine, began to live each day with tremendous clarity and love. When it was nearly the end Joe finally got up the courage to ask Christine the question: "What does it feel like to live each day knowing you are dying?" She smiled, raised herself up on one arm, and then asked him, "Joe, what does it feel like to live each day pretending that you aren't?"

One of the most powerful questions for focusing is asking yourself: "What would I be doing with my time if I knew I had only six healthy months to live?" It can immediately cause you to reorganize your priorities.

Focus is the beginning of power.

When Jesus, your personal Coach, looks at you, he will ask you one question: "What do you want me to do for you?" That was the question he asked again and again in his ministry—whether he was addressing a Roman soldier anxious about the failing health of his assistant, or a woman who had been suffering a hemorrhage for twelve years. "What do you want me to do for you?"

Jesus, the prism and focus of God, is asking you to focus now. All the power is there. All the goodwill is there. All the intent is there.

It is up to you to decide, and focus, on who you want to be and what you want to be about in this world.

NOW WE SEE ONLY REFLECTIONS IN A MIRROR . . .
BUT THEN WE SHALL BE SEEING FACE TO FACE.
—1 CORINTHIANS 13:12 (NJB)

One day Sherlock Holmes and his assistant, Watson, went camping. As the night wore on, Sherlock woke up, leaned over, and asked Watson, "What do you see?" Watson responded, "Sherlock, I see the North Star, which has helped guide us to this spot. Beyond that I see the Big Dipper and the tail of Orion. I also can make out the edges of the Milky Way and know that there are universes expanding beyond that."

Watson was about to continue his rapturous explanation when suddenly Sherlock elbowed him and hissed, "Watson, you idiot, someone has stolen our tent!"

The multiple real–life applications of this story are apparent. Watson was rhapsodizing about the beauty of the universe, while Sherlock the detective was concerned with the crime that made their new view possible.

Jesus once described himself as coming "like a thief in the night." I love the idea of his coming to steal our tent—the tent of our limited perspective—the tent of our fragile and segmented understandings—the tent that we think is keeping us safe, but is really just keeping us from seeing the universe.

Like children huddled in a tent in the back yard, we talk to each other in the light of our little flashlights, considering ourselves bold adventurers—but we haven't even explored beyond our own yard.

If only we would open our eyes to new ways of relating, seeing, and doing. If only we would focus not on the tent that has been stolen, but on our suddenly expanding view of the universe. Watch out, oh you who desire growth.

Jesus will steal your tent.

QUESTIONS: How big is your tent? How limiting is it? What is the value of this kind of "thievery"?

_____

_____

_____

_____

_____

_____

_____

Dear Lord, thank you for stealing the tent of my small—mindedness and limited thinking. Help me realize that nothing is lost, but much more is gained, when you steal away my oh—so—comfortable limitations. Amen.

MARY HAS CHOSEN THE BETTER PART.
—LUKE 10:42 (NRSV)

Planned abandonment means learning how and when to say no, as well as cultivating the discipline of saying no. Because we live in a day and age when opportunities are endless, and "acres of diamonds" lay everywhere at our feet, we need to be able to understand what to pick up and what to put down.

Jesus understood this and demonstrated it when he put down the hammer in the carpenter shop and picked up his walking stick. Being a carpenter was something he did very well, but there was something higher and more unique that he could do better than anyone else. He went toward that "occupation," and the world was forever changed.

Planned abandonment doesn't mean walking away from something that is difficult or isn't working anymore. Planned abandonment means choosing between good and great, between better and best. Planned abandonment means that you are able to say "no" to all that glitters and discern what truly shines. Once you understand the difference, you are on your way to fulfillment.

When Mary chose to leave her kitchen duties in favor of listening to Jesus, she was praised for her planned abandonment. She decided to let lesser things go in order to choose the higher part.

Jesus practiced planned abandonment.

QUESTIONS: What opportunities are confusing you right now? Name specifically the choices you are facing. Which one of those can you do better than almost anyone else? Which one of those fits squarely in line with your personal mission? Which one of those is in context with your economic engine and resources? Why must you and I learn to say "no"?

Dear Lord, Jesus could have stayed very busy as a carpenter or even as someone who could turn stones into bread out in the wilderness. He gave up the mundane in order to follow the path that was his alone. Help me to follow the path that is mine alone. Amen.

Keep Your Focus

Let your eyes look straight ahead,
And your eyelids look right before you.
—Proverbs 4:25 (NKJV)

No matter what was going on in Jesus' life, he kept his focus. It never wavered. Whether people were praising him with palm fronds or whipping him with cords, his focus remained the same.

He came to do the will of his Father, no matter what. Whether he was at a party or a funeral, a meeting or a prayer breakfast, he always stayed true to what he came here to do. He practiced focused thinking and kept growing in wisdom and favor until such a time as he was able to affect a far greater change.

It is very easy in this world of distractions and 24/7 information streams to stray off track and lose your focus. Knowing what you came here to do—and being determined to do it, no matter what—will give you more power than you can imagine.

Jesus kept his focus.

QUESTIONS: What is it in your life that you won't allow anyone or anything to disturb? What are some of the distractions, or off–balance maneuvers of other people, that are affecting you? How many distractions can you eliminate? How many distractions do you actually invite?

_____

_____

_____

_____

_____

_____

_____

_____

_____

_____

_____

_____

_____

_____

Dear Lord, you always kept your focus, no matter what.
Please help me to keep my eye on you at all times, for you are my life,
my joy, my purpose. Amen.

I HAVE NOT COME TO BRING PEACE, BUT A SWORD.
—MATTHEW 10:34 (NRSV)

I recently purchased a statue of a woman who is wearing a robe. She is barefoot. She has a laurel wreath around her head. In one uplifted hand she is holding a flaming torch. In her other hand she is holding a sword.

I often picture her in my mind when I have a difficult decision to make. She represents wisdom to me—lighting the way to those who seek, yet armed with a sword for cutting away what is false. Wisdom is about both, and that is sometimes a hard lesson to learn.

If I had to choose one of the principles and skills that most helped set me free, it would be that of learning to use the sword.

Jesus was a master at cutting away what was false . . . whether it was the hypocrisy of the Pharisees or the illegitimate relationship of the woman at the well. He was adamant that people be unbound and set free. He said, "No!" to the devil three times in the wilderness, and again when Peter tried to get him to change the road to his destiny. His silence when he was on trial cut like a knife into the hearts of those who were falsely accusing him out of their own fears.

I am certain that if you took the time, became very still and quiet, and asked in prayer, "What do I need to cut away from my life?" the answer would come to you. The question is: Are you willing to make the cut?

Jesus will teach you to use that sword.

QUESTIONS: What needs to be cut away in your life? Are you willing to make the cut? Why or why not? Imagine for five minutes what it might feel like to be free from that bondage.

When I work with young people, I ask them to do this exercise: Pretend that Steven Spielberg has optioned the rights to your life story. He intends to make a feature film about you and has commissioned three writers to submit scripts to him. One script will be about your life as it is now, as if nothing changes. The second script will contain one change of some sort—either you meet a new person or you move to a new place. The third script is the most outrageous of all—you become a totally new person—perhaps the one you always wanted to be—doing the things you always wanted to do. What would that script look like?

If you can fill in the blanks on that one, you have imagination.

If you can see the blanks being filled in, you have faith.

And if you have faith, you have your new reality.

Jesus defined reality.

QUESTIONS: Which old stories and old excuses do you drag with you? What would it be like if you could be handed a new script today? Would you take it? Do you think that you are predestined to mediocrity?

Dear Lord, you are the Author of reality.
Teach me what mine is—in your name. Amen.

Be Asked Open-Ended Questions

Who do you say that I am?
—Matthew 16:15 (nkjv)

To me, any and all transformation takes place with the help of the questions. We can sit and read or hear a lecture all day long, but never really take in the material. When we are called upon to answer questions about the material, that means some "registration" has gone on.

Jesus was famous for his questions. For example, here are a few of the learning questions that Jesus posed:

"Do you want to be healed?"

"Who do you say that I am?"

"Will you wait with me?"

"Philip, how shall we feed these people?"

"Why do you call me Lord, Lord, yet do not do the things I say?"

One only has to read the Gospels again to realize how much Jesus loved dialoguing and talking about the things of God.

In our rush to seek certainty, we shut out wonder. In our desire to know, we fail to understand what can come only from exploring open-ended questions, getting caught in the tumble and whirl of them, and eventually finding our way out.

Isn't life really an open-ended question?

Whom, then, shall you serve?

Jesus asked open-ended questions.

QUESTIONS: Who engages you in dialogue? Who issues pronouncements to you? To which person do you feel more connected? Why do you think Jesus, Son of God, enjoyed open-ended questions so much?

_____

_____

_____

_____

_____

_____

_____

_____

Dear Lord, I love talking with you, thinking with you, exploring with you.
Thank you for having an open mind, full of questions of discovery. Amen.

IN THY LIGHT SHALL WE SEE LIGHT.

—PSALM 36:9

Probably the fundamental source of any human condition can be traced back to this one question: Where is the source of light?

Jesus was intent on helping people identify their source of light. When he asked the rich young man to go and sell what he had and give the rest to the poor, he was saying, in essence, "Look to your source of light. And don't let it be money."

Yet I have found that anytime I am having a problem, or when I coach people through their own personal obstacle courses, one of the first things that needs to be discerned is where the light is coming from.

I wonder if Jesus was talking to the artist in each of us when he said, "The lamp of the body is the eye. If therefore your eye is good, your whole body will be full of light. But if your eye is bad, your whole body will be full of darkness" (Matthew 6:22–23 NKJV).

Sobering words. Author Kim McMillen wrote in her book *When I Loved Myself Enough*, "I learned that when I am feeling pain it is because I am living outside the truth."

Remember where your light is coming from, and then you can begin to see even ashes as a garland in disguise.

QUESTIONS: Where is there emotional pain or confusion in your life today? Could it be that you are looking to another source of light for inspiration, and it is falling short?

Dear Lord, help me to remember that you are my Source of light
in every situation, even when I seem to be sitting in darkness. Amen.

DO YOU WANT TO BE HEALED?
—JOHN 5:6 (CEV)

I am always amazed at how consistently Jesus assessed the readiness of his "clients" before he took them on. "Do you want to be healed?" seems like a throwaway question to a man who had been lying around on a mat for most of his life. Yet Jesus didn't want to just "de—mat" him unless the man himself could admit that he was ready.

People who have turned from therapists into coaches say the major difference between therapy and coaching is that therapy can keep people stirring their stuff for years, never making progress. Yet with coaching, the total emphasis is on "Where do you want to go next?" Good coaches don't want to waste any time, theirs or that of their clients, if the heart and mind aren't ready to move forward.

In Tucson there is a church where people meet on Sunday mornings, then proceed immediately out into the community to feed the homeless, paint over graffiti, or do other good deeds. They call this experience "workship" (www.workship.org). I love the sound of it.

Jesus as a Coach is ready to go to work. Are you?

QUESTIONS: Where in your life are you like a passive pumpkin that has a happy face, but no feet to go anywhere? Where in your life have you become bored and boring? What actions would a casual observer identify as determining your readiness for learning and for life? Are you ready to go to work?

Dear Lord, when you come to me and ask if I want to be healed, I say,
"Yes." When you come to me and ask if I want to live, I say, "Yes." I am ready,
Lord. Take me, guide me, cut me, show me what it means to be really alive.
And most of all, carve me new feet. Amen.

HAVE AN INDIVIDUALIZED EDUCATION PLAN

YAHWEH, YOU EXAMINE ME AND KNOW ME,
YOU KNOW WHEN I SIT, WHEN I RISE,
YOU UNDERSTAND MY THOUGHTS FROM AFAR.
—PSALM 139:1–2 (NJB)

A wise coach understands that not everyone can be handled the same way. Nor will all people respond to the same incentives.

When it comes to coaching, a cookie–cutter approach doesn't cut it. Each person is too individual to respond to a one–size–fits–all plan. Anyone who has ever been a parent knows this inherent truth about children. What works with Suzie might not work with Sam, no matter how closely related they are. Yet our educational systems—as well as our business leadership paradigms—often assume that one size fits all.

Jesus knows every hair on your head . . . and was with you in the womb before you were born. Why not consult with him every day to find out not only why you were made, but also what exactly he had in mind for you to be and do when he created you?

Jesus will give you an Individualized Education Plan.

QUESTIONS: What challenges do you currently face? Could it be that they are all individually and specifically designed for your growth? Which part of the growth don't you want? If you turn away from your current challenges, where do you expect your growth to come from?

Dear Lord, you have designed an individualized set of challenges for me, specifically designed to help me grow into the fullness you have for me. Help me not turn away from what is before me, but move toward it with faith, trust, and fearlessness. Amen.

HE ENTERED JERICHO AND WAS GOING THROUGH
THE TOWN AND SUDDENLY A MAN WHOSE NAME WAS
ZACCHAEUS MADE HIS APPEARANCE; HE WAS ONE OF
THE SENIOR TAX COLLECTORS AND A WEALTHY MAN. HE
KEPT TRYING TO SEE WHICH JESUS WAS, BUT HE WAS
TOO SHORT AND COULD NOT SEE HIM FOR THE CROWD;
SO HE RAN AHEAD AND CLIMBED A SYCAMORE TREE TO
CATCH A GLIMPSE OF JESUS WHO WAS TO PASS THAT
WAY. WHEN JESUS REACHED THE SPOT HE LOOKED UP
AND SPOKE TO HIM, "ZACCHAEUS, COME DOWN."
—LUKE 19:1–5 (NJB)

Imagine Zacchaeus's surprise when Jesus looked up in the tree and said, "Zacchaeus, I see you. Come on down from there and let's start interacting one on one." Jesus says the same thing to each of us.

I have a unique, one–on–one relationship with Jesus. My relationship with Jesus does not and cannot look like your relationship with Jesus, or it wouldn't be unique.

When I first began to fall in love with Jesus, I was a teenager. I decided that we would have nicknames for each other, and we still do. I also requested that we have a little personal ritual—that whenever he is thinking about me, he is to send me a ladybug. Since that time I have been amazed and delighted at how inventive and romantic and thoughtful my Lover can be.

You can do this, too. One friend has an agreement with God about white butterflies. (Joan of Arc was said to have this agreement, too, and was often seen surrounded by white butterflies as she marched off to war.) Another friend has an understanding with God about finding pennies where she least expects them. She tells the story of how every day, she will always find a penny and know that God is thinking about her. One day she was in the hospital facing surgery, and she realized that for the first time in twenty–six years, she had gone all day without finding a penny from heaven. Then an orderly walked in and said, "I found this penny right outside your room. For some reason, I needed to bring it to you." God was saying to her, "I see you. I love you. I'm here."

QUESTIONS: Do you have a little love ritual with God? If not, why not? If so, what is it? Do you believe that God sees you right where you are? Do you believe that you are worthy of a special ritual? (You are!)

Dear Lord, thank you for ladybugs and bright shiny pennies, and for the love you shine so generously on all of us every day. I love you. Amen.

HAVE FUN

MY SOUL SHALL BE JOYFUL IN MY GOD.
—ISAIAH 61:10 (NKJV)

Good coaches keep things moving, interesting, and fun, and Jesus modeled that consistently in his behavior with his team. No two days or conversations were ever alike, whether they were having a picnic or casting out demons.

Jesus kept the flow of conversation relevant and timely, inserting key questions at specific points that made the disciples stop, think, and apply.

As he and his team watched the numbers of people multiply on the shore, Jesus turned to Philip and asked, "Where will we get enough food to feed all these people?" (John 6:5 CEV). It was a major and timely learning opportunity for Philip, who then had to consider how to answer the question.

Jesus, Coach, was a master at asking the tickling question . . . the one that seemed to have no apparent answer. He kept their minds in motion and made it fun. That was one reason they followed him, and one reason they will follow you.

QUESTIONS: Do your associates eagerly await the next visit with you, or dread it? What question might Jesus, Coach, ask you about a situation you currently are facing? What are you doing to encourage Jesus as a Coach to want to hang around you?

Dear Lord, as Creator of the universe you have a mind that never stops thinking and growing. Help me be more open to having fun with you and engaging you quickly and constantly on a daily basis. Amen.

BLESSED ARE THOSE WHO HEAR
THE WORD . . . AND KEEP IT!
—LUKE 11:28 (NKJV)

When Jesus said to Peter, "Drop your nets and follow me," he didn't say, "Mañana." He meant, "Now!" When Elisha met Elijah, he immediately took action—slaying his oxen and burning his plow on the spot in order to follow his new calling (I Kings 19:20, 21). When Joseph was told in a dream to take Mary and baby Jesus to Egypt to escape the wrath of King Herod, he bundled them up immediately and headed out the door (Matthew 2:13, 14).

One hallmark of highly effective people is that they have a sense of urgency about the importance of even the smallest task. Yet all too many of us operate in sort of a mind fog that seems to tell us to "slow down, take it easy, don't sweat the small stuff." Small stuff not acted upon becomes big stuff that consumes you. (This is not to confuse worry with action. In fact, one of the greatest antidotes to worry is taking action—now.)

Time—efficiency experts tell us to handle a sheet of paper only one time. Act on it, file it, or throw it away. Don't let it just lie there, accumulating dust. Too many of us do that with our thoughts and ideas, however. We let them just sit there, accumulating dust, and then complain when someone else acts on them.

Procrastination seems like a harmless and benign habit. But the truth is, procrastination is deadly. It is costly. And Jesus said it can cost you everything.

Jesus will always encourage you to take action toward the good. And that means now!

QUESTIONS: What action that you know you need to take are you currently avoiding? Why? If procrastination were the loser in you talking, what would the winner in you say?

Dear Lord, your wonders never cease. Your patience is unending.
Yet there is a time for everything good that needs to be done,
and that time is always now. Help me eliminate procrastination in my life
so that I can see you, right now, more clearly, rather than have
you floating hazily in the fog of my tomorrows. Amen.

Use Your Greatest Strength

YOU WILL USE A TALENT OF PURE GOLD
FOR THE LAMP—STAND AND ALL ITS ACCESSORIES;
AND SEE THAT YOU WORK TO THE DESIGN WHICH
WAS SHOWN YOU ON THE MOUNTAIN.
—EXODUS 25:39–40 (NJB)

God was very specific about the materials and design that were to be used in the construction of the tabernacle. Craftsmanship and quality were paramount, and the work was to be done according to the design shown to Moses on the mountain. I like to think of this passage as it applies to building teams, companies, and organizations as well. We are to engage the finest craftspeople, allowing them to use their most pure "talents," and have them follow a design given to them from on high. Does this really happen?

The Gallup organization recently surveyed more than two million workers in 101 companies around the world. One question was this: "Do you get to use your greatest strength every day at work?" Eighty percent said that they do not get to use their greatest strength every day at work. What a waste of time, energy, and talent!

Imagine instead what we could do organizationally and teamwise if people's highest gifts were identified and unleashed.

Jesus went from being a carpenter to being a preacher. I often try to imagine what went through his mind the day he finally lay the hammer down and walked out the door, closing the shop for the very last time.

The essential thing is to realize what your strengths are and then refine them.

Jesus doesn't teach about weakest links. He teaches about finding our highest callings and strengths, and going after them with all our hearts.

Jesus used his greatest strength.

QUESTIONS: How could it be that skills and strengths might not be the same? Do you know your greatest strength? What is it? What would it be like to be able to use your greatest strength every day?

_____

_____

_____

_____

_____

_____

_____

_____

Dear Lord, help me see where my light is truly lit by you, and then set it on a lamp stand, not under a bushel. Amen.

WHAT DO YOU WANT FROM ME?
MY HOUR HAS NOT COME YET.
—JOHN 2:4 (NJB)

In coaching sessions I've observed that many clients want to do things perfectly right out of the gate. You and I might have emerged perfectly from the womb at birth, but even if we did have all body parts intact, the whole process for most of us was a bloody, painful, and at times a screaming mess.

The problem with our culture, which worships success and achievement, is that those states are not really states at all, but more like parts of a bumpy, ugly, and very uncertain process.

When Jesus did his first public miracle, by all accounts it wasn't really his idea. His mother asked him to help solve a problem at a party, and reluctantly he did so. We learn from the gospel account how rough a beginning it was. Yet Jesus did what he was asked to do, even if it wasn't the ideal time and place, according to his original plan.

Jesus was willing to have a rough start. Are you?

QUESTIONS: Do you tend to want to do things "right" the first time? Could it be that you are really just procrastinating and using other "obstacles" as an excuse not to act? Can you name others who got off to a rough start? (Abraham Lincoln, for example, lost his first two elections for public office, but won the third.)

_Dear Lord, you are willing to work from chaos and formlessness
to do your best work. Help me do the same. Amen._

BALANCE

MY DEAR FRIEND ROBIN WOOD shared with me a story that I want to pass on to you. She was invited to go ice–skating with her son, his friends, and their moms at the local ice–skating rink in Cincinnati, and the three women hit it off instantly. Inspired by the recent winter Olympics, all three of them were attempting to do spiral spins and swirls.

Yet Robin said that she took one spin on the ice and immediately collapsed upon herself. Another mother, Cecilia, did a little better but quickly lost her balance in the swirling and also tumbled into a heap. Jennifer, however, easily negotiated a perfect swirl and spin, even though she had never been on the ice before. When the other two mothers looked up at her in awe and asked how she did it, she replied, "I was trained as a ballerina. I learned how to keep my balance." When they asked her the secret to balance, she replied, "I was taught how to find my 'center,' and whenever I begin to feel off center, I instantly return to it."

How simple. How profound. Until we know where our "center" is, we will be wobbly, off–balance, and probably at odds with the world and ourselves. Once we hit that "sweet spot," we can return to it again and again. Keeping your balance means being able to swiftly and surely deal with temptations, as Jesus did. Keeping your balance means not being swayed by the cheers of the roaring crowd, wanting you to be something you are not. Being centered means being able to turn the other cheek and answer not a word, just as Jesus did. Being centered means that you can die at any time and still know that you died doing God's will, just as Jesus did.

The world is trying to find its center—through artificial highs or artificial means. Being centered—oh, the power of that! You know it when you see it. You'll know it when you have it. And once you attain the balance of being "centered," you will always know how to find it again, just as Jesus did.

This section is about balance—the one thing that people often are lacking, even when they seem to have it all.

HAVE HELP TO FIND YOUR BALANCE

SEEK FIRST THE KINGDOM OF GOD . . .
AND ALL THESE THINGS SHALL BE ADDED TO YOU.
—MATTHEW 6:33 (NKJV)

Watching the news will drive anyone to distraction, partly because of the headlines that scroll along the bottom of the screen while the anchors present the news. It would seem that our cultural belief is that if we can get enough information fast enough, we'll get it right. Unfortunately one only has to hear the news to understand that we are not getting it right, but rather are getting it wrong constantly. Wisdom is needed even more than information, and wisdom comes from balance.

Jesus taught us how to find our balance: "Seek first the kingdom of God . . . and all these things shall be added to you."

How simple balance is—if we know where we stand and what we are looking for.

QUESTIONS: Why is it so easy to lose our balance these days? Why isn't "information" the answer to the balance question? How can seeking first the kingdom of God help you find your balance? Why is it so difficult for people, especially women, to "have it all"?

Dear Lord, help me understand that you are my center of gravity. Help me choose wisely when other lives are affected. Help me discern ambition from calling, and heart's desires from consumer's call. Amen.

I WILL NEVER LEAVE YOU NOR FORSAKE YOU.
—HEBREWS 13:5 (NKJV)

Recently a friend and I went to the New Mexico state fair. As we were walking among the games, we came upon "The Pirates Ladder." To win, all we had to do was climb a twelve–foot ladder that was set at an angle and stretched over airbags. But when my friend tried it, she flipped over immediately the first time and only got up three rungs the second time. Then the attendant let me hold the ladder steady for her, and she was able to make it up.

As my friend laughingly conceded that the task was too difficult for her to accomplish without help, she asked the attendant how he did it and made it look so easy. He smiled and lifted his shirt to reveal a set of six-pack abs. "Balance isn't in your head; it's in your guts," he said and then turned to the next customer.

When Paul said "all things work together for good for those who love God, who are called according to his purpose" (Romans 8:28 NRSV), he was reminding us that if we ask, God will indeed hold the ladder for us as we make our way toward the goal.

Jesus showed us how to walk the ladder. He did it standing straight up, and he did it on his knees. And in the Garden of Gethsemane, when his mind was begging him to take the easier, lower road, Jesus showed us that spiritual balance doesn't come from your head—it comes from the midst of you—the midst of you that we commonly refer to as "guts."

Jesus held the ladder.

QUESTIONS: What ladder are you facing? Are you trying to do it alone? Have you asked Jesus to hold the ladder for you? Do you trust him to do that? Can you still trust him to help you, even when you flip over and fall? Where does your "balance" come from?

Dear Lord, thank you for holding the ladder for me. Give me the guts
to keep climbing this challenging ladder you have placed in front of me.
And help me remember that, no matter how many times I flip over or fall,
all of your life, all of my life, is by your design. Amen.

DO SUCCESSION PLANNING

THIS NIGHT THY SOUL SHALL BE
REQUIRED OF THEE.
—LUKE 12:20 (KJV)

Jesus began his succession planning almost from day one. Knowing that his time on earth was short, he began telling his followers that they would not always have him, and that they needed to pay attention to what he was doing, and how, so that when he left, they could do even greater things. He told them: "Most assuredly, I say to you, he who believes in me, the works that I do he will do also; and greater works than these he will do" (John 14:12).

While Jesus was still walking the earth, he consciously and pointedly gave the keys to his kingdom to Peter, naming him his representative. He also commissioned the apostles to be his voice and hands and feet on earth (Matthew 28:19, 20).

From the cross he named John the Beloved as his successor in the family: "John, this is your new mother. Mother, this is your new son." With his dying breath he was demonstrating the importance of taking care of those who are left behind.

Jesus will have you think carefully about your succession planning.

QUESTIONS: What legacy are you leaving behind to others in terms of "soul work"? How much planning are you doing for your life on the other side?

Dear Lord, I am so caught up in trying to lay up my riches on earth rather than in heaven. Help me think about whom and what I will leave behind, and what I am laying a foundation for in heaven. Make me ever mindful of how temporary and fleeting is this dream of a life. Amen.

Let your "Yes" be yes and your "No" be no.
—JAMES 5:12 (NRSV)

When James wrote, "Let your 'Yes' be yes and your 'No' be no," he was teaching several important concepts. The most obvious concept was the importance of keeping your word, or having integrity, but he was also talking about the habit of justification that so many of us use to our detriment. Oftentimes where there is a multiplication of words, there is a lack of clarity and purpose. If you don't believe me, read statements by politicians; they seem to cover all the bases while never quite making it home with their points.

A weakness of justification is that instead of clear communication, you just have multiplication of words. "I did this because . . ." can quickly turn into some form of excuse. And the longer the tail, the easier the animal is to catch. Jesus said the truth will set us free. When you know what the truth is, you are called upon to speak it clearly and without justification.

Another reason to avoid justification is that people who are manipulative by nature often intentionally keep people talking so they can insert a phrase of sentence that will lead the conversation into the area they want it to go. Jesus didn't stand and justify who he was before his accusers. He never gave a lengthy, detailed explanation about who he was or what he did. He just did it. He just "was."

"Let your 'Yes' be yes and your 'No' be no." Those who learn how to do this move forward faster because they move in the power of the truth.

QUESTIONS: When and where do you find yourself justifying your actions? Would you say that this is a sign of strength or weakness? Spend the next few days noticing when and where people begin to justify or obscure their actions and thoughts. What might be their motives? Once you have sought wisdom around an issue and made up your mind, experiment for the next week not justifying your actions, but simply letting them stand, because you do.

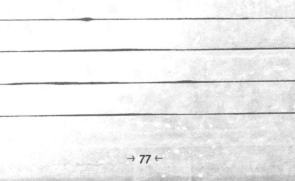

Dear Lord, help me to be more clear in my decisions and my decision—making capability. Help me not give those who would manipulate or deceive any extra or unnecessary words to use against me. Amen.

And God will wipe away every tear
from their eyes; there shall be no more death,
nor sorrow, nor crying. There shall be no more
pain, for the former things have passed away.
—Revelation 21:4 (NKJV)

Jesus looked at the little girl who lay still on her bed. "She is not dead; she's sleeping," he said calmly. Here he offered the family a change of perspective that led to a different outcome.

"Tear this temple down and in three days I will raise it up again," he said. Here he offered a change of perspective on the temporality of life and the power the people felt they had to permanently destroy it.

Jesus does the same for us. When he promises that every tear shall be wiped away, he is teaching us that somehow we are in a play that is going to have a happy ending, no matter what it looks like now.

You may be smack dab up against the hardest stone and biggest step of your life, thinking that you do not have the strength or skill set necessary to overcome it.

Yet Jesus, your Life Coach, is standing right beside you, saying, "Beloved, how would you look at this problem if you knew you could fly?"

QUESTIONS: What situation are you facing right now that has you all tied up in knots? How do you think a bird might view your situation? How can you help others gain a new perspective when they face seemingly insurmountable difficulties?

_____

_____

_____

_____

_____

_____

_____

_____

_____

_____

_____

_____

_____

Dear Lord, you said we were made of spirit, not flesh.
Help me remember to keep the spiritual perspective on all my trials,
knowing that you are beside me, and you see and know the
happy ending that is mine. Amen.

HEAR OUTRAGEOUS REQUESTS

WHOEVER BELIEVES IN ME
WILL PERFORM THE SAME WORKS AS I DO MYSELF,
AND WILL PERFORM EVEN GREATER WORKS.
—JOHN 14:12 (NJB)

Jesus came not to reinforce your comfort zone, but to set your old, small-minded ways on fire.

He doesn't ask you to just take a step here or there—he asks you to leap tall buildings in a single bound. His requests will cause you to leave behind maybe everything that you thought you knew. Are you ready?

Jesus went from the fetal position to living and dying full out—with arms outstretched as wide as they could go—and he asks the same of you and me.

He also said, "Whosoever shall seek to save his life shall lose it" (Luke 17:33 KJV). In other words, if you try to preserve your ego identity, your time on earth will be wasted and empty. But if you are willing to give up the ground of everything you think you know, and follow the way that he will show you, you will be given blessings beyond your wildest imaginings.

It is one thing to ask God for what you want. Real change happens when you ask what God wants for you.

That's when transformation occurs.

Just think about the transformations that took place all around Jesus of Nazareth.

He turned fishermen into fishers of souls, prostitutes into honored heroines, tax collectors into counselors, physicians into poets, and murderers into church leaders.

Jesus took the bread and broke it, and about five thousand were fed that day. Jesus will take the bread of your life and ask simply, "May I break this with you?" If you nod and say, "Yes," you will be multiplied in ways you never dreamed of (or you can just keep your sticky old Spam sandwich).

QUESTIONS: What outrageous requests is Jesus, your Coach, making of you? What if what he's asking really could come true? What if the only thing keeping it from happening is you? What would happen if you released the brake and decided to go for the ride?

Dear Lord, you are the builder of roads and the knower of roads.
Help me trust you—just to simply trust you and say "Yes,"
when you say, "Let's go!" Amen.

RESPECT YOUR FRAGILE THINGS

MY HOUSE WAS DESIGNATED A HOUSE
OF PRAYER FOR THE NATIONS;
YOU'VE TURNED IT INTO A HANGOUT
FOR THIEVES.
—MARK 11:17 (MSG)

Jesus was intentional about his work. He did not heal all of
the people in Jerusalem. He did not raise all of the dead. He did
not try to be all things to all people. He knew his mission, and he
stuck to it. He was also very conscious about his boundaries.

In the morning when Mary saw Jesus after his resurrection,
he told her, "Do not touch me." Yet later, that very same afternoon,
he allowed Thomas to plunge his hands into his wounds. Part of
guarding your fragile things is recognizing when and where and how
to raise and lower your personal boundaries at appropriate times.

Jesus took time regularly to draw apart, pray, and be refilled
for the draining work that he was to do each day. His fragile thing
was his unique, intense, one—on—one relationship with God, and

he did not let others trample on or interrupt that time. Prayer time, meditation time, alone time—this is one way to guard and respect your fragile things. Jesus taught us to respect that or else we cannot fly.

QUESTIONS: What would you say in your life is your most fragile thing? Who or what is stepping on it? Why have you been allowing that to happen? What could be the consequences of your not reclaiming it? Imagine what your life can be when you allow your fragile thing the time and space it needs.

_____

_____

_____

_____

_____

_____

_____

_____

_____

_____

_____

Dear Lord, you created me with a need for you. When I am apart
from you, I can do nothing—no matter how busy I may seem. Call me back
to the fragile place—the sacred space of us—those intense
breath—to—breath moments when just you and I are together. Amen.

GOD ORDAINED THAT A WORM SHOULD ATTACK
THE CASTOR–OIL PLANT—AND IT WITHERED.
—JONAH 4:7 (NJB)

If there is one thing that many of us desire in these chaotic and uncertain times, it is order. But people who believe God is frozen in stone are either ignoring or forgetting the radical, messy, "thinking on your feet and with your heart" style of leadership that Jesus embodied.

Jesus was born in a barn, not in a palace. He was placed not on fine linens, but on straw. He was surrounded not by physicians, but by shepherds and immigrants.

He grew up poor—or at least no wealthier than middle class. He did not fit the pictures of magnificence he was supposed to. And then, to top it off, he hung out with sinners, tax collectors, disabled people, and fishermen (not the group a mother would probably choose for her firstborn son). Christ was quite comfortable with chaos. In fact he seemed to create it everywhere he went.

As my grandfather used to say with a smile, "He created a stir wherever he went."

God's love is sometimes annoying. Things will not always go according to your plans. Jesus loved to laugh, loved to throw unconventional parties full of messy and unconventional people. Aren't you glad that you are invited, too?

Having a bad hair day? Maybe Jesus just rubbed your head.

QUESTIONS: Where in your life are you trying to avoid chaos? Where might God be in the midst of it? What does the term "messy spirituality" mean to you? When has Jesus messed up your hair?

Dear Lord, things don't always go the way I want them to.
Help me realize that your divine and loving order is behind
and underneath it all. And that you sometimes might mess up
my hair just to say, "Loosen up. I love you." Amen.

LEAVE REGRET BEHIND

ONCE THE HAND IS LAID ON THE PLOUGH,
NO ONE WHO LOOKS BACK IS FIT FOR THE
KINGDOM OF GOD.
—LUKE 9:62 (NJB)

Perhaps one of the most oft–quoted sayings I heard last year was, "Don't die with the music still in you."

When Jesus called out to the fishermen, "Follow me, and I will make you fishers of men," he was saying, "Follow me, and you will live a life free of regrets. Follow me, and you will live all the music that is in you."

Regrets are about things we wish we had done differently. Yet I believe that if we just take time to sit and project into the future a little bit, we can shape a life that is free of regret.

Carl Jung once said, "Nothing affects the life of a child so much as the unlived life of its parent." You would not believe how this phenomenon of "unlived lives" is revealed to have shaped so much of our own existence. Take a moment right now for yourself, and identify what was your father's or your mother's unlived life. Once you identify it, you might see how much of your own life has been shaped by that regret . . . by the things your parent wanted, but was unable to do, whether because of circumstance or choices they made or failed to make.

Taking that into the future, what "unlived life" are you facing?

Jesus talked about this when he said, in essence, "Don't go out and build a bigger barn. Go out and build a bigger life."

QUESTIONS: Based on your life up to this point, what are your regrets? Based on your life going forward, what might your regrets be? Name three actions you are going to take today to make sure that doesn't happen.

Dear Lord, you did not die with the music still in you.
Help me do the same. Amen.

HONOR YOUR ANCESTORS

HONOUR YOUR FATHER AND YOUR MOTHER
SO THAT YOU MAY LIVE LONG IN THE LAND.
—EXODUS 20:12 (NJB)

I was shocked when I read a statement that our Western culture is the only one that blames, rather than honors, our ancestors. While it is wise to examine the patterns of our parents' behaviors, both negative and positive, ultimately we do ourselves a favor when we are able to bless and honor them, somehow, some way.

The fifth of the Ten Commandments is: "Honor your father and your mother, that your days may be long upon the land" (Exodus 20:12 NKJV). This commandment is the only one with a · guaranteed blessing attached to it.

Jesus honored his mother when he saw to it from the cross that she would be taken care of after his death. "John, this is your new mother now. Mother, this is your new son," he said as his life ebbed away from him.

Respect. And honor. We must honor those who came before us, or we cannot move forward. And we must honor those who will follow us by living centered and earth—friendly ways.

Jesus honored his mother even from the cross, making sure that she was taken care of. And he lived his life with every breath, trying to do the will of his Father. No, Jesus did not blame his ancestors for his problems. Neither must we.

QUESTIONS: How are you honoring your mother and your father? What is the difference between boundary—setting and honoring? Why is it important to walk slowly sometimes in the footsteps of those who have gone before? Whom are you blaming for your problems today? If you shifted from blame to wonder, which ancestor would you take to "show—and—tell" and why?

Dear Lord, you created me from a multitude of possible DNA strands. Thank you. And thank you for choosing perfect ancestors for me—those who could show me what I need to learn in this life so that I may serve you more. Amen.

HE POURED WATER INTO A BASIN
AND BEGAN TO WASH THE DISCIPLES' FEET.
—JOHN 13:5 (NRSV)

When Joan of Arc was granted any request she wanted upon helping the Dauphin ascend his rightful throne, she asked for only two things.

One request: "Please pay off the debt of my uncle and friend who borrowed money to buy me my horse."

"Done!" said the exuberant king. "What else?"

"Don't tax the people of my village for the next four hundred years."

"Okay," said the king, gulping this time.

Her requests were honored. This leader thought not of herself, but of her people. She did not lord it over others.

Jesus, knowing that he was God and that he was about to go to God, knelt and washed his disciples' feet. Unlike all too many executives and CEOs who send their people out first to the slaughter, Jesus went forward to meet his executioners, telling them to let the people go and take only him.

Jesus, Lord of lords, saw himself first and foremost as a servant.

Great leaders do the same.

QUESTIONS: Where do you use your power to make sure that you avoid suffering, unmindful of what others are going through? Where in your life has pride caused you to fall? Where is pride lurking in your life now, sticking its foot out with a hidden smile?

Dear Lord, what a hard lesson. For me. For all of us.
King of the mountain is a slippery place. Help me take
the lowest place, and in so doing, honor you. Amen.

Know the Difference Between Archetype and Stereotype

DO NOT KEEP JUDGING ACCORDING TO APPEARANCES; LET
YOUR JUDGEMENT BE ACCORDING TO WHAT IS RIGHT.
—JOHN 7:24 (NJB)

The difference between archetype and stereotype is subtle but important. An archetype is a character that revolves around a universal theme, such as a journey or challenge—perhaps of a hero trying to find his way home—while a stereotype offers a one-dimensional view of a character in a setting, such as a woman doing the dishes. Researcher Gerald Zaltman argues that in order for marketers to build their brands, they must tap into the universal understanding of archetypal journeys and not settle for stereotypes.

Jesus was a master at delving into the unconscious "journeys" of his followers. When he offered the fishermen a chance to become "fishers of men," he was changing them from stereotypes of simple working stiffs to archetypes—embarking on a life-changing and, at times, life-threatening journey.

I am convinced that one of the greatest challenges facing society today is the tendency to stereotype others and thus miss the depth of the journeys that they are on.

The mind sorts in terms of stereotypes. The heart deals in archetypes. And that is where wisdom is to be found.

Jesus was able to look at the prostitute and see her not as the stereotype she seemed. He saw her as a woman who was about to embark on an epic journey into the depths of her soul, through forgiveness, recognition, and repentance.

Stereotype or archetype? Jesus knew the difference. He calls us to as well.

QUESTIONS: Which groups of people most anger you? List as many of them as you can think of. Why do they make you angry? Can you view each of them as a hidden hero on a secret journey to his or her own redemption, saved by the grace of God? Who might see you as a stereotype? How wrong would they be? Define your own epic journey, realizing that you are not alone.

Dear Lord, we are truly strangers in this land on our way home to you.
Help me understand that some of us get there more quickly
and more easily than others, and that you have a plan for each of us
if only we will listen. Amen.

LEARN A NEW WAY DUSTING

BUT WHATEVER CITY YOU ENTER, AND THEY
DO NOT RECEIVE YOU, GO OUT INTO ITS STREETS
AND SAY, "THE VERY DUST OF YOUR CITY
WHICH CLINGS TO US WE WIPE OFF AGAINST YOU."
—LUKE 10:11 (NKJV)

Jesus never stayed in a place where he wasn't welcome. Nor did he force his gifts on anyone who didn't want them. It showed the ultimate respect of God for people's free will, even when that will is misinformed. Leaving people alone in this misery was perhaps the hardest thing Jesus had had to do. But he did it. And so can you.

There is something quiveringly pure about Christ, and it is this: He never sold off pieces of himself to the highest bidder. Take me, or leave me, he said. But be willing to face me.

Having Jesus as your Coach may cause a few doors to be slammed in your face, but if you are willing to dust off your shoes and keep moving, your feet will be dancing soon enough.

QUESTIONS: Where are you currently not being received? Is it at work? At home? In your family? How much dust is in your house—the house of your inner life?

Dear Lord, let's get out some dust cloths today. Help me see
my way clear to lead a dust—free existence, surrounded by people who
receive me fresh every morning, just as you do. Amen.

KNOW THAT HE IS DRIVEN BY A DESIRE TO SEE YOU SUCCEED

[LOVE] BEARS ALL THINGS,
BELIEVES ALL THINGS, HOPES ALL THINGS.
—1 CORINTHIANS 13:7 (NRSV)

Two aspects of successful coaching include setting high standards and being passionately interested in seeing your client win. Jesus demonstrated both qualities.

He walked around his world seeing and seeking those who could be better, do better, live more fully. He noticed the man with the withered hand, and he joined his belief to the man's belief that indeed it could be well. He noticed the invalid by the pool of Bethesda, who had somehow been overlooked for thirty-eight years. Jesus spoke only a few words to that man, and that man got off his mat and walked (John 5:5).

When he said, "I came that they may have life, and have it abundantly" (John 10:10 NRSV), he was talking about you and me—he was talking to you and me. His entire being, his total focus, his entire life, was about seeing you and me succeed.

Wherever you are, whatever your circumstances, you must know that Jesus desperately wants to be your Coach, and he is motivated by nothing more than seeing you succeed, in every sense of the word.

QUESTIONS: Have you ever had someone in your life who was passionate about seeing you succeed? Who was that person, and how did it make you feel? If you didn't, how did that affect you? Do you believe that individual saw you, or was he or she only trying to live vicariously? Can you visualize Jesus as your Coach today, looking at you and seeing unending possibilities? Can you see him beside you even now, asking how you want your life to be better?

Dear Lord, you came to earth so that I and anyone who heard
your voice could respond and win at this game called life. Help me to
receive and believe the fact that your goal and heart's desire is only for my
good, and then help me listen and respond to your leadings. Amen.

> HOW BEAUTIFUL YOU ARE, MY BELOVED,
> HOW BEAUTIFUL YOU ARE!
> —SONG OF SONGS 4:1 (NJB)

If Jesus came to tell us anything, it is that ours is not an angry Father. God is not waiting to punish us; he is the eager Father, watching and waiting every day for us to come home. And when we do, what will he do? Throw a party to celebrate our return . . . to celebrate his love for us.

Before you can accept that Jesus wants to affirm you, you need to accept the foundational basis of a God who loves you. Not many of us can do that.

When you enter into a coaching relationship with Jesus, you will be surprised at how affirming he really is. He will lovingly notice your strengths and encourage you in them. He will cover you with blessings and joy and celebration, and thus bring your performance to a new level of divine excellence. Affirmation is the nature of your Coach. Get ready to accept it.

QUESTIONS: Are you in relationships that are affirming or degrading? Do you fear God, thinking that you will be punished if you enter into a closer relationship? How do you beat yourself up when no one else is watching?

Dear Lord, you created me in love. Help me believe
and receive your loving words to me. Help me rise with you into all
I can be. Help me see myself in your eyes. Amen and amen.

PRODUCTIVITY

SCRIPTURE GIVES US beautiful passages about how important productivity and fruitfulness are to both God and humans. The first commandment we receive in the book of Genesis is "to be fruitful and multiply." The prophet Ezekiel offers us a beautiful image of a river that gets deeper and wider: "Along the bank of the river, on this side and that, will grow all kinds of trees used for food; their leaves will not wither, and their fruit will not fail. They will bear fruit every month, because their water flows from the sanctuary. Their fruit will be for food, and their leaves for medicine" (Ezekiel 47:12 NKJV). Jesus said that those who abide in him, and sink their roots deep into his love and his being, will be fruitful.

All our busyness often masks a misconception of what it means to be productive. Productivity isn't about doing more and more, or even about accomplishment. Does a tree "accomplish" bearing fruit? Or is the fruit merely a manifestation of what was inside the tree all along? Fruit also comes in due time, looks different in different stages, and is good to behold and to eat. Are your deeds—those that are produced by your busyness—the same?

In this section we'll look at how Jesus can help you increase your productivity—mostly through "being."

COME ALIVE WITH NEW POSSIBILITIES

YES, I KNOW WHAT PLANS I HAVE IN MIND FOR YOU.
—JEREMIAH 29:11 (NJB)

Sometimes I picture Jesus as a trapeze artist, dangling from a moving swing, reaching out to me eagerly, calling me to leave my comfort zone. If I choose to make the leap, he will catch me. If I choose to stay where I am, I cannot then honestly say, "God didn't answer my prayer for a better life."

Yet I hear people say that all the time. And when I hear that, I wonder if Jesus is still dangling and swinging patiently in the circus tent, waiting for them to believe he will catch them when they let go of the trapeze they cling to.

Jesus' life was about turning water into wine and dancing with people who used to be lame. He said, "Wipe off the dust from your feet." Don't hang around negative people. Don't believe the lies that you are worthless or unimportant. Don't buy for a minute the illusion that your money will comfort you more than the relationship you can have with me. Shift your orientation away from sorrow and pain and toward the light of laughter and dance and joy.

Follow me, and I will take you places you never even knew existed.

Follow me, and we will climb mountains and get through valleys and come out of them on top, laughing, living, holding each other, into eternity.

This is the Jesus, the Coach, that I know. What is he to you?

QUESTIONS: Is your life more like a funeral dirge than a dance right now? Why might that be? Would you be willing to lift up your eyes to the hills, or do you prefer to keep them turned down into the valley? When was the last time you took a risk in the direction of your dance? How comfortable can you be, for how long, hanging upside down on your trapeze anyway?

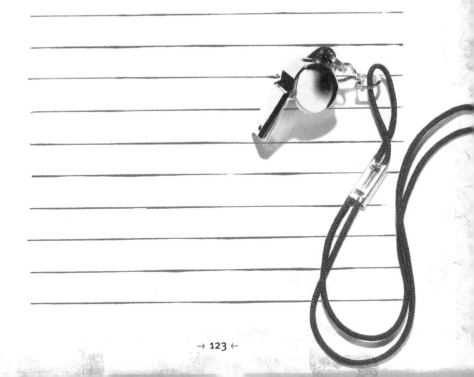

Dear Lord, you are the Lord of the dance, of life, of all possibilities.
Help me turn my eyes toward you and see in them all that I can be, can do,
can learn, can live, in this relationship with you. Amen.

UNDERSTAND RELATIONSHIP ECONOMIES

"YOU SHALL LOVE THE LORD . . . [AND] LOVE YOUR NEIGHBOR AS YOURSELF." ON THESE TWO COMMANDMENTS HANG ALL THE LAW AND THE PROPHETS.
—MATTHEW 22:37–40 (NRSV)

Imagine if your life focus became all about developing and treasuring happy memories and fulfilling relationships. How wealthy would you be?

Undergirding every principle that Jesus taught is the importance of your relationship to God, to others, and to yourself. He said it was the sum of all wisdom, all law, all prophets. Yet daily we trample over people to get to money, power, fame, or glory. Jesus said, "What does it profit you if you gain the whole world and lose your own soul?" (paraphrase of Mark 8:36). If ever there were a way that the soul would be defined, it would have to be in terms of its relationships.

How is your soul doing these days?

Jesus wants to know.

QUESTIONS: What do you think is meant by the term "relationship economy?" If your stock portfolio fell into the negative range, who or what would determine your wealth? What groups of people have you, consciously or unconsciously, decided are not worthy of being "related to"? Which groups did Jesus say were unworthy?

*Dear Lord, help me remember that in your world, relationships are not everything; they are the **only** thing. Help me remember that my net worth is determined by my heart's work, especially with others, in your name. Amen.*

Not Receive Borrowed Armor

SAUL DRESSED DAVID IN HIS OWN ARMOUR;
HE PUT A BRONZE HELMET ON HIS HEAD, DRESSED HIM
IN A BREASTPLATE AND BUCKLED HIS OWN SWORD OVER
DAVID'S ARMOUR. DAVID TRIED TO WALK BUT,
NOT BEING USED TO THEM, SAID TO SAUL,
"I CANNOT WALK IN THESE; I AM NOT USED TO THEM."
SO THEY TOOK THEM OFF AGAIN.
—1 SAMUEL 17:38–39 (NJB)

King Saul tried to give young David his armor—convinced that the young shepherd boy didn't have a chance against Goliath on his own. David allowed them to fit him with someone else's armor—the king's. Yet within minutes he knew that it wasn't him, and he shed it in order to be himself, depending solely on his relationship with God.

Jesus said that the yoke he fashioned for you would be easy, and the burden would be light. That is because he is a custom tailor, if you will, and does not desire or accept that you wear someone else's clothes.

You need no other armor but what he provides for you. And it will fit perfectly. He will not give you borrowed armor.

QUESTIONS: Where in your life are you living through someone else—either in blame or in longing? What might it feel like to actually walk in your own set of armor? If you examine the failures of your past, how many of them might be attributed to the fact that you were wearing borrowed armor?

_____

_____

_____

_____

_____

_____

_____

_____

_____

_____

_____

Dear Lord, help me realize that you are my Cloak and my Shield.
I need no other armor than the truth of your love. Amen.

WHEN I WAS A CHILD, I USED TO . . .
THINK LIKE A CHILD; BUT NOW THAT
I HAVE BECOME AN ADULT,
I HAVE FINISHED WITH ALL CHILDISH WAYS.
—1 CORINTHIANS 13:11 (NJB)

Jesus taught accountability and participation in life. When he said, "Follow me, and I will make you fishers of human souls," he was talking about expanded being and thinking—not as a child looking for its next mouthful, but as an adult seeking to shape the world.

As my friend Jackie Brewton says so eloquently, "We live beneath our Divine Privilege." With that privilege comes responsibility.

Yet I am often guilty of asking God merely for things . . . for success . . . for protection . . . for safety for myself and my loved ones . . . for a painless life and an ease—filled passing into an even better place. When I do that, am I a Christian, or merely a mouthy papoose, strapped onto God for dear life, wanting only to be fed and cared for?

Jesus will rock your world. And you will begin, as an adult, to learn what it is to be mature in an uncertain, uneven, unfair world, where you and I are called to be the eyes and arms and ears of Christ . . . taking up our part in the true Christian community of compassion and social action rather than riding on a playground of carousels pushed by leaders with their own adult agendas.

QUESTIONS: Where in your life are you still acting like a child? How do you think God views that? When does "faith" really begin to look like childlike begging? What is the difference?

Dear Lord, help me become a Christian who keeps you company rather than one who requires a pacifier and diaper bag. Amen.

WITH JESUS AS YOUR LIFE COACH, YOU WILL
PRACTICE POSITIVE CONFRONTATION

IF YOUR BROTHER DOES SOMETHING WRONG,
REBUKE HIM AND, IF HE IS SORRY, FORGIVE HIM.
—LUKE 17:3 (NJB)

Jesus was a master at the art of positive confrontation. It is only when you and I are willing to ask the hard questions, first of ourselves and then of others, that we will begin to move into the higher levels of true prosperity and fulfillment.

Jesus often began his "coaching sessions" with a positive confrontation: "Do you want to be healed?" "Where is your husband?" "Who do you think I am?" He did not mince words or always try to be polite when it came to getting to the truth of things. He stated over and over again, "The truth shall set you free."

Unless and until we learn the art of positive confrontation, change will not take place—either in our individual lives or in society. There are conversations that you probably know you need to have, but are afraid to have. What are they?

Jesus will teach you positive confrontation.

QUESTIONS: What courageous and positive confrontations do you need to have in your life today? What is the difference between a positive confrontation and an out–and–out attack? Whom can you get as your ally and role player to rehearse this courageous and confrontational conversation? Do you confuse being nice with being true?

Dear Lord, you know that I need to have some hard talks with a few people. Give me the courage and the follow—through to do so. Amen.

HE TOOK BREAD, GAVE THANKS AND BROKE IT.
—LUKE 22:19 (NKJV)

Jesus, as a man, never created something from nothing.

Jesus used water that was already there in order to make wine. He used a fish's mouth to deliver a coin to pay Caesar's tax. He fed the five thousand by first taking a piece of bread that had been offered to him, giving thanks, breaking it, and then distributing it to the people gathered all around.

Two principles are key here. The first is that surrender of what you have is always required. Had the wedding caterers not been willing to bring jars of water, there would have been no wine. Had the little boy not given up his lunch, there would have been no picnic. So, whatever God is asking you to do, do. Surrender. Give it up.

The second principle to remember is that whatever you offer up is going to change form. It may look broken and/or smashed to smithereens in the process, but it will be multiplied.

The resources you began with will not be recognizable to you when you are through. Their essence might be the same, but they will be multiplied. Whether it is a picnic basket with food left over, when you thought you had enough only for yourself, or a boat that is about to go under with all the fish that are flopping on its deck, you will be amazed at what the Lord will do for you, through you, if you offer him what you have.

Your bread will be multiplied.

QUESTIONS: What resource do you have right now that feels inadequate? What will happen if you offer it up, as the little boy did at the feeding of the five thousand?

Dear Lord, take what I have, such as it is, and multiply it according to your will. I am prepared to stand amazed. Amen.

SOME FRIENDS DON'T HELP, BUT A TRUE FRIEND
IS CLOSER THAN YOUR OWN FAMILY.
GALATIANS 1:10 (CEV)

Many Christians have a notion that "if God is in this, the doors will swing open." Although that is many times true, sometimes it is not.

The danger of teaching the saying as if it were a hard—and—fast spiritual truth is that sometimes God's will does not take the path of least resistance. Remember, the path of least resistance is often downhill.

For example, Moses had to go to Pharaoh seven times in order for the patriarch to get the message that it was time to let the Israelites go. If Moses' coach at that time had believed "if God is in this, the doors will swing open," Moses would have headed back to the desert, only to herd sheep for another forty years.

When you consider the words of Jesus, you will be amazed at how often he asked people to swim upstream. Jesus told the fishermen to undo tradition and throw the net on the other side of the boat. Jesus told Peter later in a dream to take the message of good news to the Gentiles, a message that was changing a tradition of "exclusivity" of nearly three thousand years. Jesus told his disciples to swim upstream, be kind to their enemies, and pray for them. He told his disciples to swim upstream when he declared that they were to seek not the things of the world, which rust and can be stolen, but to seek first the kingdom of God, an invisible state of being, and store up treasures in heaven. Jesus' every message was "swim upstream."

Jesus swam upstream.

QUESTIONS: Where is your Coach asking you to swim upstream? What seems so difficult about it? What might be the reward if indeed that is where the treasure lies?

Dear Lord, thank you for teaching me that your ways are higher
than my ways. Thank you for challenging me not to take
the easy way out . . . not to just walk through any door that swings open,
but to seek your will and guidance in all things. Amen.

Show Yourself Friendly

A MAN WHO HAS FRIENDS MUST HIMSELF
BE FRIENDLY, BUT THERE IS A FRIEND
WHO STICKS CLOSER THAN A BROTHER.
—PROVERBS 18:24 (NKJV)

So many people grew up with an image of an angry, thundering, lightning—scattering God that now it is difficult for them to imagine God as being friendly. Yet one only has to glance through the Gospels to realize how friendly Jesus really was. He was always reaching out to others and expecting the best from and for them.

"Hi, Zacchaeus! Why don't you come down out of that tree and let's have supper together?" he called out good—naturedly to a man who others mocked and scorned. Jesus showed himself friendly.

"Hi, there," he said to the woman at the well. "What are you really looking for here?" He spoke first and in a gentle manner to a perfect stranger. He reached out to her.

Consider his recruiting methods. "Hi, there! Want to follow me?" And they did!

The very first psalm states, "Blessed are those who do not sit in the seat of scoffers or cynics." Yet haven't we as a society been in danger of that? Friendliness and optimism were hallmarks of Jesus' personality. He was willing and able to speak the truth. Yet his resilience and popularity with the crowds showed him to be a friendly man, one who loved to celebrate and bring life wherever he went.

Jesus showed himself friendly.

QUESTIONS: When you see a stranger coming around the corner, are you wagging your tail in anticipated friendship, or hunkered down, expecting mistreatment? Where in your life could you be more friendly and reach out to others more than you have been, even in little ways? What might be the benefits of doing that?

Dear Lord, the fact that the sun rises on the evil as well as the good shows that you are in spirit friendly to all. Help me be the same. Amen.

BLESSED ARE . . . YOUR EARS BECAUSE THEY HEAR!
—MATTHEW 13:16 (NJB)

One of the hallmarks of good coaches is that they listen more than they speak. In fact, the ideal ratio of listening to speaking when being a coach is ten to one. In other words, ninety percent of a coach's main activity is listening rather than speaking.

Reflective listening takes place when you not only pause and consider what has been said, but are able to repeat it back accurately to the speaker. *Reflexive* listening is waiting simply for your chance to insert something into the conversation.

The book of Proverbs is full of sayings about the value of silence. One of my favorites is, "Answer not a fool according to his folly" (26:4 KJV). In other words, you don't have to express an ignorant opinion just because someone else has.

Jesus was a man of few words. When he walked up to a person on the street, he asked, "What would you like me to do for you?" And then he listened for the answer.

Jesus knew how to listen.

QUESTIONS: How much do you really listen to other people? Define reflective listening. Define reflexive listening. Why is listening a form of surrender? Why is surrender a form of listening? What would the world be like if more people listened rather than shouted at each other?

Dear God, Jesus said, "Thank you, Father, for listening to me."
I want to say the same. Amen.

IT WAS AT THIS TIME THAT JESUS CAME FROM
NAZARETH IN GALILEE AND WAS BAPTISED IN THE
JORDAN BY JOHN. AND AT ONCE, AS HE WAS COMING
UP OUT OF THE WATER, HE SAW THE HEAVENS TORN
APART AND THE SPIRIT, LIKE A DOVE, DESCENDING
ON HIM. AND A VOICE CAME FROM HEAVEN, "YOU ARE
MY SON, THE BELOVED; MY FAVOUR RESTS ON YOU."
—MARK 1:9–11 (NJB)

Jesus was a man of the desert. He knew that few things in that
arid region were more valued and vital than water. Indeed, he
described himself as Living Water to the woman at the well. Jesus'
first recorded miracle was turning water into wine. Some of Jesus'
favorite times were on or around the Sea of Galilee, and in one
verse we are told that "even the winds and the seas obey him"
(Matthew 8:27).

Yet what amazes me about him was that he was willing to get
wet so that we could be lifted high and dry.

When you step into God's will, there can be a feeling or perception that you are in control . . . on top of things. God's words and ways are just sort of nibbling at your ankles. You can choose to get out of the stream at this point if you are afraid or if the water is too cold or you become uncomfortable.

Yet the deeper you go into God, the deeper the water gets.

Jesus was willing to change from one state to another . . . from being a carpenter to a preacher and healer . . . to enter into lands that were not friendly to him, familiar to him, or easy on him. Yet he took that step. He was willing to get wet, and that is when his "reign" began.

QUESTIONS: Where are you maneuvering to stay in your comfort zone? What water is swirling around in front of you, stirring up unnamed fears? Who is pounding on the diving board behind you right now wanting a turn to jump in?

Dear Lord, help me get wet! Amen.

ANYONE WHO HAS EARS SHOULD LISTEN!
—MATTHEW 11:15 (NJB)

Coaching is the fine art of meeting the need for consistent feedback that is wired into the human brain. Even God gave feedback to Jesus, saying, "This is my beloved Son, in whom I am well pleased." Jesus told of the wealthy man who said to his faithful stewards, "Well done." When his disciples came back to him with their wins and losses, Jesus gave them feedback about how they needed to improve: "This kind only comes out through prayer and fasting." They told him their failures. He gave them feedback.

Jesus, your Coach, will give you feedback.

QUESTIONS: Who gives you feedback now regarding your performance? What kind of feedback is it? How could Jesus give you specific feedback?

_Dear Lord, you give me feedback in many ways—through Scripture,
through friends and family, through pastors and associates,
through bosses and coworkers. Help me listen to the ultimate
form of feedback that you promised, which is the peace that passes
all understanding. I seek to do your will. Amen._

TAKE ACTION

IT IS NOT ANYONE WHO SAYS TO ME, "LORD, LORD,"
WHO WILL ENTER THE KINGDOM OF HEAVEN,
BUT THE PERSON WHO DOES THE WILL OF MY FATHER
IN HEAVEN.
—MATTHEW 7:21 (NJB)

Jesus said: "No man, having put his hand to the plough, and looking back, is fit for the kingdom of God" (Luke 9:62 NKJV). In other words, he was saying, "Get on with it." God's will for our lives often is revealed only in retrospect. We take action and then look back and see how everything came together . . . how this person crossing our paths led to this happening, and so forth. God's will for us is so immense, and so complex, that it could never be revealed to us in a Fed Ex package or an e—mail. We must go out and meet it!

Jesus seized the moment.

QUESTIONS: Where are you just waiting for God to act? What if your actions are the paths that miracles need to take in order to come true? How can you know you are doing God's will?

Dear Lord, teach me to seize the moment, as Jesus did,
and always do good, wherever I find it. Amen.

BE WILLING TO ASK FOR HELP

WILL YOU WAIT AND PRAY WITH ME?
—MATTHEW 26:38

Jesus was willing to ask for help. For example, we are all familiar with the times he asked for help from up above: "Dear Father, hear my prayer. Heal this child," or "Raise Lazarus." He always acknowledged that he needed help from his Father to do anything. Yet he was equally comfortable asking for help from down below, that is, from his earthly peers: "Will you follow me?" or "Will you wait with me?" One of the most amazing qualities about Jesus was his willingness to show vulnerability.

Jesus spoke the truth at all times so that people could trust him. His willingness to ask for help—to show vulnerability—is yet another reason people were so willing to follow him. He indicated that he had a need for them in his life, and that allowed them the terrific feeling of being needed.

God was open enough and vulnerable enough to ask Adam to help him name the animals in the Garden. Perhaps he hoped that if humans felt some ownership of the creation, we might feel more involved and responsible for it.

Yet even God was there displaying a need and desire for teamwork—for a combined effort and contribution to a larger whole.

Know–it–alls are annoying to everyone, even and especially to God. Jesus asked for help.

QUESTIONS: When and where have you recently asked for help? Was it a large or a small project? What might be five benefits of being willing to ask for help with the challenge facing you now?

Dear Lord, help me get over my pride enough to realize
that something is missing. Help me ask for help from others to see
what it is, that we all may feel the richer for it. Amen.

THINK INSIDE THE SOLUTION

GOD SAID, "LET THERE BE LIGHT;
AND THERE WAS LIGHT."
—GENESIS 1:3 (NKJV)

When Jesus looked at the man with the withered hand, did he see the withered hand? I often ask this question in seminars, and people hesitate to answer, thinking it is a trick question.

The answer is obvious. Of course Jesus saw the withered hand, or he wouldn't have known that healing needed to take place. But he thought inside the whole hand, and that led to its transformation.

They say an acorn has to move the equivalent of ten tons of earth in order to see its first daylight sprout above ground. Would it have made it if it looked at the problem?

Jesus said, "The kingdom of God is within you" (Luke 17:21 NKJV). He also said, "I am the vine, you are the branches" (John 15:5 NJB). Natural connection. Easy flow. Why do we make things so hard?

Jesus thought inside the solution, which is where we always are.

QUESTIONS: Where in your life are you looking at the problem rather than thinking from inside the solution? How often do you see yourself as being separate from God? Where is your ego in terms of the "problem"? If you didn't have an ego, would there really be a "problem"?

Dear Lord, help me understand how natural solutions flow as long as
I remind myself where I am and where I am meant to be. Amen.

WHY DO YOU SEEK THE APPROVAL OF MEN
BUT NOT THE APPROVAL OF GOD?
—PSALM 105:2 (NJB)

How clearly are we really seeing our world? When we look at our lives, what do we see? What does Jesus see?

Jesus cares because Jesus sees. And he teaches us to see. Not just what is going on around us . . . not just the daily parade of calendar items and to–do list check–off sheets . . . but the wondrousness of creation.

Jesus didn't deny the existence of tears, the pain of death, or the sorrow of loss. He looked at it and through it.

He capped everything with a sense of wonder—of knowing that God's love was in and through it all—the underpainting on the canvas that would ultimately shine through. He taught, with every singing breath, that God's love is the creator and finisher and companion on life's wondrous journey.

So, your heart . . . where is it? Is it all bound up and constricted with the demands of the day? Or are you willing to take it, pumping complex mess that it is, and place it into the fingers of a tiny baby's hands?

Jesus taught us the meaning of wonder.

QUESTIONS: Have you forgotten a sense of wonder in your life? What situation that is seeming to paralyze you right now might be seen differently if you looked at it with a sense of wonder rather than fear? What would it mean for you to give your life into the hands of a child—to begin to see your world through a child's eyes?

_Dear Lord, you continually marveled at creation—the lilies of the field, the
dew on the grass, the fields ripe for harvest. Help me to see the world
through a child's eyes today—with a sense of joy and wondrous participation
in, and appreciation of, this incredible world—this incredible life. Amen._

REMOVE THE CHIP FROM YOUR SHOULDER

DON'T WALK AROUND WITH A CHIP
ON YOUR SHOULDER.
—PROVERBS 3:30 (MSG)

In order to have an abundant life, one must have clear vision and a full, free range of motion, emotionally, spiritually, physically, and mentally. Jesus was constantly working to remove chips from shoulders among his disciples and those he taught.

"Do you think you are better than the Samaritans? Forget it."

"Do you think that a widow's mite is less than your many dollars? Forget it."

"Do you think that a person who spends money on perfume is less worthy than someone who claims to give it to the poor? Forget it." (This woman knew the difference between pour and poor.)

"Do you think that you can get to heaven with your heart full of judgment and anger? Forget it. God doesn't even want to see you in the temple until you have dealt with the chip on your shoulder."

Jesus calls for a rigorous "full body scan" in order to set you free.

Indeed, Jesus is the only one of us entitled to have a "chip" on his shoulder, but all too many of us do.

Jesus will remove the chip from your shoulder.

QUESTIONS: Where do you have a chip on your shoulder? As a clue to discovering where it is, what triggers you suddenly into an inappropriate rage? What group or groups of people have hurt you in the past? How might that have caused you not to see clearly others who look like them? Are you willing to submit to a spiritual "full body scan" with Jesus? If so, when?

*Dear Lord, right now, sit with me and look into my heart. Help me
clear out old scars from the past, and give me a new heart and new eyes
to view every person, every situation, with a fresh perspective of hope,
optimism, and the clarity of your all—encompassing love. Amen.*

GIVE NO WEIGHT TO NEGATIVE THOUGHTS

HOW BLESSED IS ANYONE WHO REJECTS THE
ADVICE OF THE WICKED, AND DOES NOT
TAKE A STAND IN THE PATH THAT SINNERS TREAD,
NOR A SEAT IN COMPANY WITH CYNICS,
BUT WHO DELIGHTS IN THE LAW OF YAHWEH
AND MURMURS HIS LAW DAY AND NIGHT.
—PSALM 1:1–2 (NJB)

Jesus was no stranger to negative thinking.

In the gospel accounts of his wilderness experience, we are told that the devil tempted him: "If you are really as powerful as you say you are, why not throw yourself off the temple?" Given that Jesus was obviously hungry and thirsty and faint from his forty–day fast, it is no wonder that negative thoughts began to rush into his mind. Notice how he immediately rebuked each one, using prememorized positive thoughts of scripture to combat the negativity: "You shall not tempt the Lord your God."

When Peter later suggested to him that he should not go to

Jerusalem (and meet his destiny) but take an easier way out, Jesus immediately rebuked the thought, recognizing that the negativity came from only one source, and it wasn't God.

Jesus dealt with negative thoughts through scripture, prayer, and surrender of himself to God. He also demonstrated the wisdom and benefits of having a fun and interesting support group and community of friends.

If you are besieged by negative thoughts, consider the benefits of all of the above, lest the negative thoughts pull you under.

Jesus gave no weight to negative thoughts.

QUESTIONS: How many negative thoughts do you have per day? Per hour? How much do you dwell on them? How might you unburden yourself from these kinds of thoughts? What scriptures or wisdom texts might help combat negative thinking?

Dear Lord, help me to be a guardian of my thoughts. Let me not
give them weight or substance, lest they become a dark cloud keeping
me from the joy and sun of your reality. Amen.

FULFILLMENT

THERE IS A SUBTLE but significant difference between success and fulfillment.

When Jesus called out to the fishermen, "Follow me, and I will make you fishers of men," he was redefining success for them. Life under his tutelage was not going to be about increasing an earthly catch (although they certainly did that, too).

Jesus' goal for you is a life fully lived. He will call forth in you more love than you ever thought you could handle—more faith than you ever thought was possible—more excitement than any roller-coaster ride you ever took.

People pay to get frightened at movies or deliberately take stimulants to boost their adrenaline. With Jesus as your Coach you won't need drugs to get high. Nor will you need to go to the movies to get frightened. This loving Coach will bring your greatest fears into the light and help turn them into stepping-stones. He will cause you to face your unfaceable issues so that you can see light as well as be light.

No longer will you need to wonder whether your glass is half full or half empty. It will be full to overflowing—with joy and contentment and "the peace that passes understanding."

King David wrote, "Surely goodness and mercy shall follow me all the days of my life: and I will dwell in the house of the Lord forever" (Psalm 23:6 KJV).

Fulfillment has many facets to it. In the following section, we will explore some of them.

> I WILL OPEN MY MOUTH AND TELL STORIES.
> —MATTHEW 13:35 (MSG)

Virtually all therapy involves helping clients associate new meanings with old stories. Whether it is Gestalt or rational emotive or Freudian, many, if not most, types of therapy involve someone listening to an old story and helping the client find new meanings in it. Only when the person has transferred from believing the old story (I am a victim) to believing a new story (this event is only helping me be a much stronger person) does real healing take place.

In the book *How Customers Think* by Gerald Zaltman, he writes that the words "store" and "story" are very similar for a reason. The mind remembers what it attaches emotion to, and by incorporating stories around facts or perceptions, the memory improves. In fact, memory gurus teach people to help remember names by telling a story around a person's name. It is a time—honored technique to link stories to memory. Do we understand that the stories we tell ourselves, about ourselves, often tend to come true?

The truth is, you and I are playing out on a daily basis the stories we believe about ourselves. Which story is that?

QUESTIONS: Based on your life results right now, which story about yourself have you been living? Do you believe that you could get—and live out—a new story?

_____

_____

_____

_____

_____

_____

_____

_____

_____

_____

_____

_____

_____

Dear Lord, I think I want to hear a new story at bedtime tonight.
Tell me the story about me—why I was created and where you would
like to see me go. I can't wait to hear it. Amen.

I WILL MAKE YOU AN OBJECT OF ETERNAL PRIDE,
A SOURCE OF JOY FROM AGE TO AGE.
—ISAIAH 60:15 (NJB)

One of the joys and challenges of having Jesus as your personal Coach is the work he will do on and with your self-esteem.

In my seminars on *Jesus, CEO*, I challenge people to find anything negative that Jesus ever said about himself. No one has yet been able to produce a word. He was able to separate the behavior of the person from the essence of the person, which is why he was able to so freely love "sinners." He told his friends that he called them brothers and sisters, not lesser beings. He told them that they would do even greater things than he was doing. He told them that they had the faith within them to accomplish anything if they asked it believing.

Jesus believes that you and he can do anything together. Your faith, combined with his power and his faith in you, can truly move mountains and release wonderful forces of blessing on this earth.

One reason that coaching shows such phenomenal returns on investment is the simple dynamic of having another person believing in you and moving alongside you with that belief.

- Jesus sees you as wholly loved and beautiful.
- Jesus wants you to see yourself as he does.
- Jesus will believe in you, even when you can't.

QUESTIONS: Who do you think you are? Who do you think Jesus thinks you are? What have you attracted into your life through your positive and negative beliefs about yourself?

Dear Lord, help me to see myself as you see me.
Help me to feel as loved as I truly am. Amen.

BE A VOICE, NOT AN ECHO

LET ME HEAR YOUR VOICE.
—SONG OF SONGS 2:14 (NJB)

As I rounded the curve heading down to the freeway, I noticed a campaign poster stuck in somebody's front yard. It read, "Vote for Susan. She Will Be a Voice, Not an Echo." I love that line.

Jesus was a man whose life changed history not only because he was the Son of God, but also because his was a unique voice, not an echo. He did not just perpetuate the way things were done. He said, "Do it differently." He did not just remind others what had been said in the past. He said, "Behold, I show you a new way of doing things . . . things that have never been done before."

Finding your voice can take a lifetime or a moment. But once you do, use it.

In one of the most moving passages in Song of Songs, the lover says to the other, "Let me hear your voice" (Song 2:14). Your voice. He wasn't interested in hearing someone else's. He wants to hear yours.

QUESTIONS: Where are you an echo? Where are you a voice? What is the danger of merely repeating information that others have fed into you? How did Jesus express a voice unique enough to change the course of history? How will you?

Dear Lord, help me find my voice and use it for your glory. Amen.

LEARN OF YOUR DIVINE CONNECTION

WHITHER SHALL I FLEE FROM THY PRESENCE?
—PSALM 139:7 (KJV)

My mission is to recognize, promote, and inspire divine connection in myself and others. The more I have contemplated and endeavored to live this mission, the more of an oxymoron it becomes because connection implies "separateness."

And the more I grow in God, the less separate I feel. Jesus said, "Without me, you can do nothing" (John 15:5 NKJV). He was speaking of the need for, and naturalness of, divine connection.

God is omnipotent and omnipresent. We are the ones whose form is temporary and changing.

How are we using our time on this planet? To do good, do evil, or just gather dust? Divine connection. I don't know about you, but I want to live this life, and leave this life, beaming light and love.

QUESTIONS: What do you hope to accomplish on this planet
before you are beamed home? Where do you see yourself as separate
from God?

_____

_____

_____

_____

_____

_____

_____

_____

_____

_____

_____

_____

_____

_____

Dear Lord, thank you for my being and my beingness. Help me to use this gift of a life, and of a time, wisely, that all may see your Light in me and you may be glorified. Amen.

BE IN A FUTURE STATE

FAITH IS THE SUBSTANCE OF THINGS HOPED FOR,
THE EVIDENCE OF THINGS NOT SEEN.
—HEBREWS 11:1 (NKJV)

One of the principles that will change your life the most is that of vision—or of being in a future state as if it were already true. Jesus said, "I tell you . . . everything you ask and pray for, believe that you have it already, and it will be yours" (Mark 11:24 NJB).

Jesus came to demonstrate and teach transformation, and faith is the transformative power of the universe.

When Jesus becomes your Coach, you will be asked to see what isn't yet seen, to move onto a bridge that doesn't seem to be there, to describe the taste of honey when you're swallowing tears.

Perhaps you've been given a vision—one that maybe you have despaired of ever coming true. No matter what the circumstances, God sees clearly the real you—the healed you—the powerful you—the prosperous you—the person you dream to be—the person you really are, prospering in that abundant life.

Now your job is to believe it.

QUESTIONS: Do you have a dream or a vision that you've given up on? What if it were still true—could be true—in God's eyes? Why would faith be an ingredient of vision? What are you doing to nurture your faith?

Dear Lord, help me get my fingernails dirty in the places where
you tell me to dig. Amen.

Understand the Power of Presence

I am with you always.
—Matthew 28:20 (nkjv)

In Psalm 17 King David wrote about his yearning to feel God's presence. I think about this verse often, for it translates the desire not to have a God who is at our beck and call, doing things for us, but to have a God that we get to simply "be with" and enjoy:

> For me the reward of virtue
> is to see your face—
> and to gaze my fill
> on your likeness.
> (v. 15, paraphrased)

All of Scripture, really, represents a yearning for the presence of God. Jesus calls us to fall deeper and deeper into the beingness of God. For in that presence, we can indeed be wonder–full.

QUESTIONS: Whose presence do you most enjoy? What qualities about that person (or those persons) actually transform you? What would it mean if you knew you could always be in God's presence?

Dear Lord, help me to stop and remember that you are indeed
everywhere—especially right here with me—in this very moment. Amen.

I GO TO PREPARE A PLACE FOR YOU.
—JOHN 14:2 (NKJV)

When I first began contemplating Jesus as a motivator of people as well as the Son of God, I was intrigued by how he was able to get people to be so open with him.

I am convinced that people followed him, and died for him, because he offered them a safe space. Not "safe" in terms of no physical danger coming to them, but a space that was safe for them to be who they truly were and could be. The space he offered them was not a building or a church, but a relationship of unconditional positive regard.

Somehow, through his words and his deeds, and the way he beheld them, they understood that all their weaknesses and past failures did not matter to him. He was not interested in their pasts—he was all about their futures.

Jesus created a safe space by defending his staff from criticism by the scribes and the Pharisees. He did it by defending the woman who washed his feet with her hair. He did it by telling the woman caught in adultery that all her accusers were gone now, and neither did he accuse her. He did it by inviting the thief on the cross to come home with him.

If only we could do the same.

When people feel safe, amazing things begin to happen. Sometimes they even get up and walk, or are able to see again.

Jesus created a safe space.

QUESTIONS: Where is your "safe" space? Where do you not feel safe? When have you felt the safest? Why is a sense of safety essential for the soul to emerge?

Dear Lord, you are my Rock, my Salvation, my Safety Net. I come to you and know that I am loved, no matter what. I come to you and know that you see all my failings and shortcomings, yet you love me anyway. I come to you praying that I will see what you see in me, and believe, and know, and grow into the person you created in such deep love and wonder. Amen.

KNOW THAT HE IS ALWAYS REACHING TOWARD YOU

YAHWEH CALLED ME WHEN I WAS IN THE WOMB,
BEFORE MY BIRTH HE HAD PRONOUNCED MY NAME.
—ISAIAH 49:1 (NJB)

I was blessed to be able to visit the Sistine Chapel in Italy with my mother. Having long seen representations of the image on the ceiling of God reaching out to Adam, I was eager to view it with my own eyes. Yet that image is one of good—bye. God is telling Adam: "You are going to a new world now—on your own." In contrast, the image that Christ brings is one of "Hello . . . and . . . welcome to a whole new world."

Scripture tells us that even the earth is groaning in labor. We are constantly moving into new areas of being, thinking, and experiencing. How wonderful to know that even when we get stuck, there is a hand reaching out to us . . . eager and yearning to bring us into a whole new world.

Jesus is reaching out to us.

QUESTIONS: Do you feel stuck in your life right now? Do you feel that you need to move? What would it be like to realize that Jesus is reaching out to you right now?

_____

_____

_____

_____

_____

_____

_____

_____

_____

_____

_____

_____

_____

_____

Dear Lord, thank you for reaching into my messy, stuck situation and working to set me free. Help me trust you enough to place my tiny hand in yours. Amen.

THE MOST EXQUISITE FRUITS ARE AT OUR DOORS;
THE NEW AS WELL AS THE OLD, I HAVE STORED
THEM FOR YOU, MY LOVE.
—SONG OF SONGS 7:14 (NJB)

My friend and pastor Dr. Tim Walker in Grapevine, Texas, shared that death must be like birth. Embryos in the womb know only darkness and rocking and silence, and enter this world reluctantly, crying in protest with their first breath. Yet when their eyes are opened, they encounter "amazement."

Life lived in the spirit, and in the presence of Jesus, is one of continually unfolding amazement. Miracles surround us daily if only we have eyes to see. Jesus will give you a new pair of eyes.

QUESTIONS: When have you entered into a state of amazement? What was happening? Describe a time when you saw something for the first time with new eyes. What was it? How did it feel?

Dear Lord, help me walk in a state of grateful amazement
at all you have done for me. Amen.

DON'T THINK YOU HAVE TO PUT ON A FUND—RAISING
CAMPAIGN BEFORE YOU START. YOU DON'T NEED
A LOT OF EQUIPMENT. YOU ARE THE EQUIPMENT.
—MATTHEW 10:9—10 (MSG)

Jesus became very clear that he was God's Word made flesh. He said, "I am the way, the truth, and the life" (John 14:6). He said, "I am the good shepherd" (John 10:14). He said, "Whoever has seen me has seen the Father" (John 14:9 NRSV). He knew that he was God's representation on earth, and he never wavered in that understanding, however difficult it made his life and his choices.

Somehow we all must be made to understand that through the miracle of spiritual transformation in Christ, we, too, become the message. No matter what words we say or how we act, it is our deeds and our being that people will remember.

Perhaps Pilate said it all when he declared, "Behold the man" (John 19:5 NKJV). With those words he was saying, "Look at him, and you will see everything that he is—without pretense, without artifice, without shame."

Too many of us are trying to be like, look like, or sound like someone else.

Yet God is calling each of us to find, and live, with our own authentic voices. If only we could be who we truly are, this world would be changed in an instant.

Jesus knew that he was the message.

And so are you.

QUESTIONS: Where and how are you trying to be someone else? If someone looked not at the words, but at the theme of your life, what would it be? How would your life change if you realized that you are God's message in your very world?

_____

_____

_____

_____

_____

_____

_____

_____

_____

_____

_____

_____

_____

*Dear Lord—wow! You have stunned me. You have exalted me.
You have shocked me. You have instilled in me the growing sense of wonder
and fear and realization that in this world, in this time, in this place,
I am your message and your messenger. Help me stay true to the note that
you created me to be. Amen.*

THE LITTLE GIRL IS NOT DEAD; SHE IS ASLEEP.
—MATTHEW 9:24 (NJB)

One of the most amazing gifts that Jesus, your Life Coach, will bring you is that of a new perspective. A reading of any of the parables in the Gospels reveals his astonishing way of looking at the world through new eyes:

- "If you have faith, even as a mustard seed, you could move this mountain."

- "You could tear down this temple, and in three days I would raise it again."

- "If you believe in me, and ask in my name, nothing shall be impossible to you."

When events beyond our control and our comprehension take place, these are the moments when eternity breaks through.

Jesus told us, "There is a time and place when no tear will ever fall again, nor any sorrow be remembered. I have come from

Dear Lord, take my hand and lead me into your light. Amen.

YOU WILL TEACH ME THE PATH OF LIFE,
UNBOUNDED JOY IN YOUR PRESENCE.
—PSALM 16:11 (NJB)

King David expressed an unbounded joy when he wrote,

My heart rejoices, my soul delights,
   my body too will rest secure,
   for you will not abandon me to Sheol . . .
You will teach me the path of life,
   unbounded joy in your presence,
   at your right hand delight for ever. (Ps. 16:9–11 NJB)

There is a joy to be had in a personal relationship with God
that the "regular" world often cannot understand. We are told that
when the Holy Spirit fell on the group of apostles, they all began to
speak in languages they didn't understand. When they poured out of
the Upper Room and into the city streets, they were so ludicrously

happy that the people thought they were drunk (Acts 2).

Jesus himself was accused of being a joyous wine bibber, and in his prayers he asked constantly that our joy might be full.

Encountering God and surrendering to him will leave you breathless, in an altered state often too beautiful to describe. This is the way Jesus feels about you. Angels shout; the party hats come out; the finest wine is opened and poured. The joy of union and reunion is what this Coach wants for you.

When Jesus is your Coach, you will feel unbounded joy, and begin to recognize the joy he feels for you.

QUESTIONS: When in your life have you been ecstatically happy? What if you could experience this feeling consistently? What is the difference between joy and achievement? You were created in joy, and to joy you will return. Meanwhile, joy on earth is available to you in ways that pass all human understanding. Are you open to it?

*Dear Lord, help me awaken to your joy—the joy you have in me
and for me. All my desire and my reward is in you. Amen.*

AND TO ONE HE GAVE FIVE TALENTS,
TO ANOTHER TWO, AND TO ANOTHER ONE,
TO EACH ACCORDING TO HIS OWN ABILITY.
—MATTHEW 25:15 (NKJV)

A card that I purchased at the Georgia O'Keeffe museum in Santa Fe, New Mexico, is in my briefcase so that I have it handy at all times. It includes a statement the artist made in reference to her unending love affair with New Mexico: "It belongs to me. God told me if I painted it enough I could have it." We all are artists in our own ways—each attempting to express ourselves on the canvas of our daily lives. The sad thing is that so often we miss our own art because we do not step back and observe where the brush strokes are going.

Now imagine if you could make a living doing every day what you most love to do. Like Georgia O'Keeffe, understand that if you paint it often enough, God will give it to you.

Jesus left the carpentry shop of his father to head out into the wilderness, teaching, healing, and preaching, urging us to come out of our boxes and reach for the sky.

Jesus painted what he loved, and he challenges us to do the same.

QUESTIONS: If someone were to interpret your brush strokes today, what would your painting portray? Why did Georgia O'Keeffe think that God would give her something if she painted it enough? What did she mean by that?

Dear Lord, help me paint what is loved, and lovable, in your eyes. Help me also understand that somehow, I am your great masterpiece, and that doing what I love the most gives pleasure to you, my Creator. Amen.

Concluding Thoughts

I learned yesterday that everyone loses twenty-one grams when they die. Whether the body is young or old, heavy or thin, something ineffable leaves it that weighs only as much as a hummingbird.

Perhaps this is what the human soul weighs, or the breath that circulates through our lungs day in, day out—from our first great gulp of air to our last soft sigh.

This is the part of you that Jesus seeks— not the weight of your accomplishments or the heft of your bank account—not even (dare I say it?) the list of your good deeds.

Jesus is looking for the essence of you— the twenty-one grams granted at birth—the twenty-one grams that may ascend into heaven when you die.

Turn your breath to him now—whisper "Yes" to him again and again—and your life will turn imperceptibly, boldly, hugely toward the ultimate, greatest, happiest "You."

Amen and Amen.

JESUS, LIFE COACH

Jesus, Life Coach Journal is based on the book by best-selling author Laurie Beth Jones. In *Jesus, Life Coach* she invites readers to learn life-coaching from the best coach who ever lived—Jesus Christ.

There was a time when only athletes had coaches. Now, everyone from CEOs to at-risk youth is being "coached." The International Coaching Federation—which began with only a handful of people—now boasts membership of over 5,000, and currently more than 150,000 people call themselves "Life Coaches." The benefits of coaching have been well documented, but having the right coach is critical.

Jesus had only three years to train the twelve disciples, yet in that time he managed to turn this ragamuffin group into "lean, clean marketing machines." Divided into four critical sections—Focus, Balance, Productivity, and Fulfillment—*Jesus, Life Coach* presents a faith-based coaching program with Jesus as the model. Delving into the principles Jesus used to transform those around him, the book offers proven strategies and countless applications for modern-day coaches.